THE TRIAL OF WILLIAM SHAKESPEARE

A dramatization of the authorship controversy in which the audience renders a verdict

THE TRIAL OF WILLIAM SHAKESPEARE

A dramatization of the authorship controversy in which the audience renders a verdict

J. Ajlouny

THE TRIAL OF WILLIAM SHAKESPEARE

**A dramatization of the authorship controversy
in which the audience renders a verdict**

Copyright © 2018, 1998
by J. Ajlouny
All rights reserved

Push Pull Press
An Imprint of:
Fresh Ink Group, LLC
Box 931
Guntersville, AL 35976
Email: info@FreshInkGroup.com
FreshInkGroup.com

Edition 1.0   1998
Edition 2.0   2018

Cover art by Anik
Cover by Stephen Geez

Performance: Any performance of this play must be licensed in writing by the publisher, including royalty arrangements. No alterations, deletions, or substitutions of a material nature may be made in this work without prior written permission of Fresh Ink Group, LLC. Authorship credit must appear on all programs and promotions in all media where space permits.

Publication: Except as permitted under the U.S. Copyright Act of 1976, no part of this publication may be reproduced, distributed, or transmitted in any form or by any means, or stored in a database or retrieval system, without prior written permission of Fresh Ink Group, LLC.

BISAC Subject Headings:
PER013000   **PERFORMING ARTS** / Theater / Broadway & Musicals
PER011000   **PERFORMING ARTS** / Theater / General
DRA001000   **DRAMA** / American / General

Library of Congress Control Number: 2018933400.

ISBN-13: 978-1-936442-75-1 Softcover
ISBN-13: 978-1-936442-80-5 Hardcover
ISBN-13: 978-1-936442-76-8 Ebooks

Playscript / Drama

No person in history, except perhaps Christ Himself, has had to endure the indignation of having his very existence challenged as often or as profusely as has William Shakespeare (or Shaxper) late of Stratford-upon-Avon. For over a hundred years now, scholars and cranks alike have seen t to question the man and his works, not because he didn't write them, but because they can't possibly bring themselves to believe that he did.

Accumulated here are the arguments for and against the proposition that The Stratfordian was indeed the author of the plays and poems attributed to William Shakespeare. All statements and all proofs are drawn from the historical record, which the playwright has painstakingly researched. Ultimately each person must decide for him or herself. In this age of reticence and disbelief, this is proving to be no small task.

Remarks from audience/participants/jurors:

"Absolutely fascinating!"

"I didn't realize the depth of this mystery."

"It's a good case... and an intriguing courtroom drama."

"Well written and well played."

"The playwright's research is impressive and his use of humor is brilliant."

"Lots of fun!" "There's not a chance in hell he wrote those plays."

Foreword

BARD BEYOND BELIEF
The Persistent William Shakespeare Mystery

By Jonathon Bate
Professor of English Literature, University of Liverpool

The annoying thing about William Shakespeare is that his life was so mundane and so unpoetic. The only raw materials he required for the creation of his plays were a grammar school education and a lifetime in the theater as an actor, scriptwriter and shareholder of the King's Men, the most successful playing company of the age. He became the most admired dramatist of his generation, but nobody expressed any surprise when in about 1612 he handed over the role of in-house scriptwriter for the King's Men to John Fletcher and retired to his hometown of Stratford-upon-Avon, where he died quietly four years later.

Seven years after that, his fellow actors—whom he had remembered with generosity in his will— put together the sumptuous First Folio of his collection "Comedies, Histories and Tragedies." His friend Ben Jonson contributed a generous prefatory poem, "To the memory of my beloved, the author Mr. William Shakespeare," in which the "Sweet Swan of Avon" was praised as a poet who outstripped the classical authors of Greece and Rome in spite of his own somewhat limited acquaintance with their works.

Over the next hundred years, Shakespeare's reputation fluctuated, the *frenchified* court taste of the reign of Charles II showing a preference for Jonson and Fletcher. But in the course of the 18th century, first in Germany and then in England, there was a reaction against the stultifying "correctness" of French taste, with its demand for tragedy to be kept apart from comedy and high culture from low. The new watchwords were "naturalness" and "original genius" – qualities found above all in Shakespeare's plays.

By the time of the Romantic movement in the 19th century, Shakespeare had become synonymous with creative genius. But Romanticism brought a new cult of the artist's life. To be a true genius one had to live on the edge, to be struck dead like Beethoven, to be mad, bad and dangerous to know like Byron, or to wander the Orient in a drug crazed stupor like Rimbaud. So it was that a motley crue of Victorian and Edwardian eccentrics set about reinventing Shakespeare in the image of the Romantic artist.

The most enduring of these reinventions has been the attempt to dress him up as a cross between Byron and the Scarlet Pimpernel. Over the years more than a dozen Elizabethan aristocrats have been dusted off and presented to the public as the true author of the plays. Americans have been especially fascinated by the bizarre pseudo-mystery. Perhaps because the only two things the British have and Americans have not are Blue Blood and William Shakespeare, it has proved all too tempting to suppose that Shakespeare was a "nobleman in disguise."

Yet their case remains unproved. While it may seem unlikely to some, the fact remains, William Shakespeare, the Warwickshire squire, was indeed the principal author of the poems and plays attributed to him. Though the evidence to prove this fact is admittedly wanting, there is absolutely no proof that anybody other than he was the true author. Yes, many names have been submitted, ranging from Edward deVere, the 17th Earl of Oxford to Francis Bacon, and even to King James 1 himself. However, not only did they nor their heirs ever claim authorship, the known facts disqualify each one. The true author of Shakespeare's works was a normal family man who retired into obscurity, tended to his own affairs and enjoyed a natural death far from the madding crowds. Now that's poetic!

© 1997 Jonathon Bate
Reprinted by permission

The Trial of William Shakespeare

A dramatization of the authorship controversy in which the audience renders a verdict

J. Ajlouny

The Trial of William Shakespeare

The Year: 1668

The Place: Court of Chancery; Abington, Northhampton

The Setting: The scene is a provincial courtroom. The bench is centerstage on a dais. The clerk's perch (desk) is directly beneath and in front of it. Two barrister podiums are situated to the left and right facing each other. An easel is nearby to hold exhibits.

Characters:

1. Tobias, clerk of the court
2. Justice Hugh Templeton, judge
3. Henry McNagg, barrister for Petitioner (producers and printers)
4. James Sparrow, barrister for Respondent (Lady Elizabeth Bernard, Shakespeare's granddaughter)

Descriptions:

The clerk is a responsible court official, a comical character, like a Shakespearean "fool";

The Judge is crusty, impatient and is suffering pain from a toothache;

The attorney for Petitioner is stuffy, polished and over-confident;

The attorney for Respondent is an earnest novice, fumbling yet endearing.

Scene One

Enter the Clerk. He is a young man, bright, organized but comical in appearance and manner. He has a feather duster in one hand and a satchel of documents in the other. He is humming or whistling contentedly. He ascends the bench, begins to dust it and tidy it up. He places the documents upon the bench and selects a docket list therefrom. He then descends to his own desk, and dusts it and his chair. He checks the quill and ink well on his desk by tapping the pen tip on his tongue. He signals his distaste, then his satisfaction that it is ready for use. After standing back and inspecting the premises, he exits, still whistling.

A stoic voice is heard reciting Sonnet 81:

> *Or I shall live your epitaph to make, Or you survive when I in earth am rotten. From hence your memory death cannot take, Although in me each part will be forgotten. Your name from hence immortal life shall have. Though I, once gone, to all the world must die. The earth can yield me but a common grave When you entombed in men's eyes shall lie. Your monument shall be my gentle*

verse. Which eyes not yet created shall o'er read; And tongues to be your being shall rehearse When all the breathers of this world are dead. ou still shall live (such virtue hath my pen) Where breath most breathes, even in the mouths of men.

Scene Two

Lights go up.

The Clerk re-enters wearing a black robe and small reddish wig. **The Judge** enters following him. The Judge is wearing judicial robes, a large white wig and is carrying a gavel. He is seated as the Clerk remains standing to the left. The Judge, after situating himself comfortably, pounds his gavel several times.

Clerk:

Hear ye, hear ye. Know all men by these presents that the Court of Chancery for the county of Northhampton, sitting in Abington is in session this 7th day of May in His Majesty's year of Sixteen hundred and Sixty-eight, Lord Justice Hugh Templeton presiding. *(Gazing upon the seated audience.)* You may be seated.

Judge:

Call the first case, Toby.

Clerk:

Calling the matter of *Revels vs. Dryden*, Docket number 162. *(Pauses)* Is anybody present for the matter of Revels and Dryden? Step forward at once. *(Pauses again.)* Nobody?

Judge:

The matter is dismissed for failure of prosecution. *(He pounds his gavel one time.)* Next case!

Clerk:

Calling the matter of *Powlet-Jones vs. The Master of Lincoln's Inn,* Docket number 245. My lord, the petitioner in this matter has sent word from Ipswich that he is unable to attend due to the present state of the Northhampton Road following the recent rains. He begs leave for a one week adjournment.

Judge:

And the respondent, where is the King's Counsel Charles Howard?

Clerk:

Petitioner states in his message that his carriage was to meet and transport Sir Charles hence from the livery at Shotswell Green. Their purpose having been frustrated by the condition of the road, he is not present either, my lord.

Judge:

In that case, let the matter stand adjourned for thirty days. By next month the mud should be dry and they'll have no excuse for failing to appear. And with a little luck they will have settled their differences, thereby saving us all the trouble. *(Pounds his gavel once, and grasps his jaw, grimacing in pain with a toothache.)* Ahhh, Neptune's daughter be damned! Toby, call the next case. *(To himself.)* Ahhh, the pain, the pain!

Clerk:
Yes, my lord. Calling the matter of *Bernard vs. The Stationer's Register*, et al., Docket number 297, being better known as the Shakespeare authorship controversy. Are the parties present? *(Muttering to himself.)* For their sake!

Petitioner's Counsel:
Present, my lord.

Respondent's Counsel:
Present and ready to proceed, my lord. *(As he stands, his papers fall from his arms and scatter on the oor. Embarrassed, he collects them while offering apologies.)*

Both counsel take their places at the respective podiums. Petitioner is a middle-aged gentleman, refined and well-learned. Respondent is youthful, inexperienced and appears nervous.

Judge:
Tobias, please read the history of the proceedings for the record. And don't dally about it.

Clerk:

No, my lord. *(He stands and clears his throat.)* The matter was first brought by Respondent Sir John Bernard, husband of Lady Elizabeth Bernard, only surviving heir to the estate of her grandfather, the poet known as William Shakespeare, late of Stratford-on-Avon in Warwickshire. It is his Sir John's claim that rights and pro ts from the printing of his wife's grandfather's poems and plays are rightfully hers. *(Pointing to Petitioner)* Petitioner represents a consortium of printers, theatrical producers, stage managers and actors whose interests are vicariously represented by His Majesty's Stationer's Register, being the licensing authority for the publication of said poems and plays. The cause was tried before a panel of magistrates September last. Judgment was rendered for the Stationer's Register largely upon the grounds that Respondent's case was unproved, he having the burden of proof in the matter. On appeal to His Majesty's High Court, it was declared that irreparable harm was in icted upon Petitioner's claim by so placing the burden of evidence. The matter has thus been remanded here to re-determine the matter of authorship with the presumption of the evidence weighted in favor of Respondent because no other claimant has come forward.

Judge:
Very good. Are the parties ready to proceed with oral arguments?

Petitioner:
Ready, willing and more than able, I assure my lord.

Judge:
And Respondent? Is he ready or must we wait until he has finished organizing his papers?

Respondent:
(Jumpig to attention.) Oh... ready, my lord, as ready as it is in my power to be.

Judge:
Very well then. Since it has been determined that Petitioner carries the burden of proof in this cause, Petitioner will present his proofs first. *(Grimacing with pain.)* Aghhh...

Petitioner:
Thank you, my lord. Permit me to preface my rhetorical remarks, my lord, with a brief observation. This case may be looked upon by novices of legal theory as an attempt to deprive the family of Lady Bernard of the legacy of her grandfather, Master William Shakespeare (or "Shaxper"

as he had apparently also been known). Let me state unequivocally that this is not the case and that is certainly not our intention. Neither I nor my clients, each of whom is a respectable businessman, has anything but the highest respect and greatest esteem for Sir John, and the Lady Bernard, on whose behalf this claim is advanced. However, her claim, while a tender one, is not borne out by the known, provable facts, as your lordship will soon discover. Moreover, her ladyship can scarcely be considered to have been denied her due, as she is in fact the sole heir to the rather substantial estate of her late grandfather, to which she is fully entailed and of which she is presently possessed. On the contrary, if there be sympathy in this cause, it must be the sympathy that men of honor feel when the reputation of honest tradesmen is besmirched by gossip, innuendo and rumor. Had matters transpired differently, on a less public path, I'm sure my clients would be only too willing to make some accommodation with Sir John. Unfortunately, no simple expediency will now serve their cause as the matter has brinked a point of principal from which they cannot stand down. I doubtless need remind my lord that when it comes to honor, men have sacrificed far more than my modest barristerial fees.

Now, my lord, if I may be permitted, I will present my case as succinctly and completely as it is in my power to do so.

The judge gestures for him to continue.

Respondent:
Objection, my lord! I have an objection.

Judge:
And what might that be, young sir?

Respondent:
Well, my lord, Sir Henry has made an opening statement.

Judge:
Yes...?

Respondent:
I claim the same right. Had he limited matters to a summation of his intended proofs I would have held my silence. However, he has colored these proceedings with issues of motivation, which, if left unanswered, might cause grave injury to my client's case. Whether this controversy is about honor or money is irrelevant. The fact remains, Sir Henry and his allied clients are attempting to rob Lady Bernard, indeed, all posterity, of

her grandfather's reputation as a poet and playwright. It seems of little importance why they seek to do this, though heaven knows, my lord, speaking of sacrifice, it is evident that men have never hesitated to sacrifice honor in the pursuit of profit.

Petitioner

Objection, my lord! Is the young barrister questioning my honor?

Respondent:

It is not *your* honor which is at stake here, Sir Henry.

Judge:

Let's get on with it, gentlemen. If we are to question matters of honor, we might as well question the nature of man. That's not going to get us anywhere, is it gentlemen?

So let us proceed. *(Grimacing in pain again.)*

Agghhh....

Respondent:

As I was saying, my lord, I request the right to answer Sir Henry's opening statement with a statement of mine own, prior to the proofs being submitted.

Judge:
It seems to me you've already done that, Master Sparrow. But your point is well-taken. Objection sustained. *(Gesturing to McNagg to commence.)* Petitioner...

Petitioner:
Looking irritated at Sparrow for having been interrupted. Thank you, my gracious lord. I detect a measure of discomfort in my lord's comportment this morning. For that matter, I will endeavor to Fulfill my task quickly and, pardon the expression, my lord, painlessly.

Judge:
Aaggghh!

Petitioner:
It seems to me, my lord, that the Respondent's claim rests upon certain documentary evidence which if true and accurate, might be sufficient to proof the case, if just barely. However, I will show beyond doubt that said documentary evidence is in fact untrue, inaccurate, and indeed, is completely unreliable to prove anything except its own sorry existence.

Just who was this Mr. William Shakespeare or Shaxper or Shaxberd, as he was variously known, anyway? Unfortunately, the record is pretty thin when it comes to documentary facts. All we know is that he was born in 1564 in the town of Stratford-Upon-Avon, was married in 1582, fathered her ladyship's late mother Susanna Hall in 1583, and at some point subsequent became attached to a ragtag assembly of players and vagabonds in London. He then apparently labored in the theater in a variety of trades until he joined the Lord Chamberlin's Players in the spring of 1594. I cannot offer your lordship a date certain because it is not known. I also cannot state with certainty what his duties were, as these are unknown as well. Some have suggested that he held horses outside the gates, others that he was a copyist, actor, stage manager or housekeeper. It is simply not known. Therefore, if he was the company's chief playwright, as is contended, this is unknown as well.

"Shaxper" had no known education whatsoever. His breeding was unremarkable. His expectations were next to nil, owing largely to his own father's fickleness and financial distress. Indeed, the man was so non-descript that even his own name is the subject of speculation. Yet a simple English lad such as this is presumed to be a great poet. It won't do!

All of the records of the age, now some three-quarters of a century afterward, reveal little if anything to substantiate such a lofty claim. He was not recognized during his lifetime by his peers nor by the aristocracy, or indeed, even by the public at large as a writer. Rather, he is remembered as a marginally successful grain dealer and landowner from Warwickshire. None of his papers have survived, and there is no record that he ever claimed to be what he obviously was not. And though he is said to have been the fountainhead of many great works of literature and the owner of interests in at least two prominent London theaters, not a single word is written about either in his Last Will and Testament, which I'm sorry to note, is the sole surviving document of which he could loosely be described as, "the author ." Yet, we are asked here to accept as fact that he was a luminary of the written word. One glance at his signatures on the will brings into question, my lord, whether the man knew how to write at all. To this purpose, my lord, I submit facsimile of the known signatures of "Willem Shaxper," so pronounced, my lord because that is apparently how he signed his name on more than one occasion. Can we ethically and morally dismiss the obvious uncertainty in the name, its various spellings and their very illegibility? *(He presents an exhibit of the signatures and displays it facing the audience.)* I think not! So stilted and child-like are they. Yet this is the hand that, if the editors of the First Folio of his works are to be believed (whom I will shortly prove are not to be believed) penned manuscripts which "scarce had a blotted line." I say again, this will not do!

Upon the gentleman's death in His Majesty's year of 1616 — I call him a gentleman because that is what he was presumed to have been, and was so described in the parish record of his death — his estate fell upon her ladyship's father, the late Dr. John Hall, to administer. Yet strangely, if not mysteriously, if the Respondent is to be believed, every shred of evidence of the alleged poet's literary effects were either misplaced, burned or otherwise lost. All of them. Not a single letter from this man of letters has survived. Not a single couplet, rhyming or not, has survived. Nor has a play, part of a play, nor indeed a single sheet of paper upon which Master Shaxper ever put pen to, survives. Yet this is the estate of a foremost English writer and it is void of anything written! But let's not end here; no, it would be wrong to leave it there. Neither books, nor quartos, nay, not even a single printed article has been discovered among his belongings. Yet these were the belongings of England's foremost literary marvel. I repeat, it will not do!

Now that the circumstances of this man's life and death have been described, let me turn to the important and somewhat delicate matter of the so-called First Folio of 1623, upon which the credibility of Respondent's case chiefly rests.

As my lord is no doubt aware, the state of the printing trade was in its infancy at the turn of the last century, which is the period with which we are here concerned. Practices which we find abhorrent today were routine in those days. Thus, literary piracy, for example, was commonplace. Printers, most of whom were also booksellers, would print books and pamphlets without regard to those who owned them. Indeed, the very notion of one's having rights in his own written words was unknown at that time.

Judge:
Yes, yes... are you almost nished?

Petitioner.
One or two final embellishments, my lord. Now, where was I? Where was I? Oh yes! As

I was saying, there was simply no recognition at the prevailing time of what we regard as *delio in publico* or " delity in publishing" as it is popularly championed — not least by and among my clients — today.

Judge:
So, what's the point? I mean, how is this "embellishment" relevant?

Petitioner:
The point, my lord, is to combat inferences by brother counsel that since many editions of poems and plays attributed to a William Shakespeare were in fact printed and that this, in and of itself, proves that he in fact wrote them. The plain truth is that the title pages of the quarto editions of the time were entirely unreliable. In the interest of time I will spare the court the dozens upon dozens of examples that have come to light of the making of false and deceptive attributions of authorship but suffice it to say that it happened regularly. Therefore it proves nothing to say that because a play or a poem was never attributed to anybody else means its authorship is definite. In that day, plays and poems were routinely misappropriated, and the fact that they were misattributed more than once to the same author does not, my lord, mean that person

wrote them. Indeed, it doesn't even prove the person was an author at all! Those who printed the several quartos of the plays, as well as those who printed the First Folio, were as guilty of this misconduct as any of them were. Accordingly, their editions will always remain suspect and can't be considered reliable in proving much of anything. To accept this logic would render unattributed poems and plays as unwritten. I repeat, it will not do!

Judge:
Very good, thank you counselor for that finely rendered statement of proofs. Now ...

Petitioner:
(Interrupting) My lord, one final point, if I may be so bold. After all, a nail isn't often driven home by a single blow.

Judge:
Pray, continue but please make your point in the manner you represented you would.

Petitioner:
Of course, my lord. Now where was .... oh yes! As irregular and shameful as the printing and book-selling trade were at that time, my lord, the business of drafting plays can only

be described as utterly inexplicable. Utterly, my lord! In fact it's been said by no less an authority as Christopher Marlowe himself, about whom no such controversy exists, that writing plays was a job for hacks and cynics and amounted to nothing more than catering to the baser instincts of the mob. In other words, my lord, one didn't have to be a writer, one only needed to be a hack and a cynic. The celebrated author Robert Greene expressed a similar sentiment on his deathbed when he called such folk "puppets." Both of these learned and eminent writers were describing, of course, these so-called playwrights, who in fact were really never anything more than lifters, purloiners and re-write men who served the selfish interests of theater owners in their relentless desire to own every play they could find a way of stealing. Moreover, dozens and dozens of plays have in them the hands of two or more, sometimes even as many as half-a-dozen different, so-called authors. Thus, a cursory review of the plays attributed to Master Shakespeare, whoever he really was, proves that every single one was based in whole or in part on the works of other writers who preceded him. Ans so — that her ladyship is not distressed, the same can be said for almost every play and every playwright of that era. These writers were mechanics, not artists; they were at best editors, not authors. They stitched plays together and so, that the players and costumes they held in common. And, being content with their role, they didn't receive credit for authorship on title pages or play programs. Nor did they hawk their wares to printers. In truth, they didn't even consider themselves as playwrights. A person can't fool others, it is said, when he is unwilling to fool himself, and these men didn't try to fool anybody. Our Mr. Shaxper or Shakeshaft, or whatever his true name was, would almost certainly blush at the suggestion that he is the author of the plays and poems with which we are concerned today. He made no claim to them in his lifetime and I rather doubt one should be made fifty-two years after his death.

Judge:
Very good...

Petitioner:
(Loudly) In conclusion, my lord, let me Briefly state that the case is a simple one. Whosoever Lady Bernard presumed her maternal grandfather to be, a man who was all but unknown

to her and of whom she does not have a single recollection he was most certainly not the author of the poems and plays attributed to "the" William Shakespeare; nor could he have been. Not only is there no evidence that he ever wrote a single thing, the evidence we do have suggests he didn't even know how to read. Yet we are expected to accept that this skeleton of a man is the biography of a literary genius. I say, my lord, it will not do! Accept this proposition, my lord, and the courts of all England will be soon be packed with petitioners of every stripe seeking to foist posthumous praise on their ne'er-do-well relations. It would be intolerable! Therefore, my lord, for the foregoing reasons I respectfully request you find in favor of Petitioners. There is no evidence to prove Respondent's grandfather ever wrote anything other than his own pathetic signature.

Judge:
Good, Sir Henry. Well put. Now we'll hear from Young Master Sparrow, if he's ready?

Respondent:
Ready my lord.

Judge:
Then proceed. Aggghhh... And please be at least as "concise" as Sir Henry *(looking askew at Petitioner)*, if you will.

Respondent:
I will endeavor to do my best, my lord, would that my oratorical skills could match those of Sir Henry. But I believe he does my clients a grave injustice by ignoring the evidence that was presented at the hearing, from which this appeal originates. I will therefore, my lord, present the facts of Master Shakespeare's authorship as they were presented at trial, one by one, in sequence, to prove beyond any doubt that, un-privileged as Master Shakespeare may have been, he was indeed the primary author of the mighty works attributed to him *(looking at Petitioner)* both during his lifetime and since his death some years ago.

Respondent proceeds to place a large chart on an easel. He positions it facing the audience.

First, my lord, we must begin where the evidence of authorship begins, in 1592. Sir Robert Greene, a poet, playwright and nationally acclaimed wit, penned an autobiographical preface to his posthumously published work entitled *Greene's Groats-worth of Wit Bought with a Million of Repentance*. In the preface, which is epistolary in style and addressed to three unnamed "University writers," as he called them, commonly supposed to have been Edmund Spencer, Thomas Nash and George Peele, Greene issues a warning that certain players of the stage are assuming roles as writers, and in so doing, are cheapening the reputation of authors such as themselves. It is clear that by 1592, Master Shakespeare had already achieved singular recognition as a playwright because of Greene's venomous remarks against him, which, my lord, I venture to suggest, were written out of envy and petty jealousy. And what did Greene write, you ask? Let me read from the manuscript directly, as only his true words can speak his true feelings:

> *"Base-minded men all three of you, if by my misery you are not warned. For unto none of you (like me) sought those players to cleave — those puppets (I mean) who spake from our mouths, those roles garnished in our colors.... Trust them not, for there is an upstart crow, beautified ed with our feathers, that with his tiger's heart wrapped in a player's hide, supposes he is as well able to bombast*

out a blank verse as the best of you. And being an absolute jack of all trades, is in his own conceit the only Shake-scene in our country."

Mark, my lord, his having called Master Shakespeare, an "upstart crow," with "a tiger's heart wrapped in a player's hide." And mark further, his jibe at the variant spelling of Master Shakespeare's name, by calling, bitterly I might add, "Shake-scene." Thus my lord, is the first column of my case erected. For Robert Greene, angry and cantankerous as he was reported to be near his death, when this bit of doggerel was penned, was in a position to know the facts *at that time.* And he has described Master Shakespeare as a writer new enough to threaten the more worthy, so-called "University writers," of the age.

Item second, my lord, is the reply to Greene's invective, in the nature of an apology, that was offered shortly afterwards by the London printer Henry Chettle, who admits to having a hand in the publication of *Greene's Groats-worth of Wit.* His letter does not name the two playwrights to whom it was addressed, but Chettle let it be known afterward that he was writing about Christopher Marlowe, whom he cared for not, and Master Shakespeare, a man upon whom he generously offers praise. Let me read Chettle's exact words, my lord, for they are highly relevant to this enterprise:

> "*With neither of them that take offense was I acquainted, and with one of them I care not if I never be.*"
>
> *(The Clerk holds up a sign for the audience which reads "Marlowe was gay!")*
>
> "*The other, whom at that time did not so much spare, as since I wish I had... I am as sorry as if the original fault had been my fault, because myself have seen his demeanor no less civil than he excellent in the quality he professes. Besides, many gentlemen have reported his uprightness of dealing, which argues his honesty and his facetious grace in writing, that approves his art.*"

I am tempted to rest my case on this statement alone my lord, so clear and truthful as it is. Mr. Chettle, whose statement is unassailable — and conveniently ignored by Petitioner — is a highly credible witness. And he attests to Master Shakespeare's "honest, uprightness and grace in writing." Yet Sir Henry insists he was illiterate. The facts, my lord, prove otherwise. But let's not end here, let's, as Sir Henry is want to do, drive the nail home.

Item third, my lord...

Judge:
Exactly how many items do you have?

Respondent:
Only a bushel full, my lord, just a bushel full.

Judge:
I advise you to make it a half bushel. Agghhh...

Respondent:
Indeed, my lord, a half-bushel's worth is all I will present, though I can assure you there will be plenty of grain remaining when I am finished.

Judge:
If I hunger for more, I'll be certain to let you know. Please proceed.

Respondent:
Of course, my lord. Item third. The narrative poems *Venus and Adonis* and *The Rape of Lucrece,* dated 1593 and 1594 respectively. As my lord is sufficiently aware, theaters are routinely ordered closed during times of plague. This is a public health measure. In February 1593, my lord, a most heinous plague descended upon London and the surrounding region. Accordingly, the theaters were closed for the following

nine months. During these times of closure, players and theater workers were forced to seek alternate employment. This included Master Shakespeare, who by this time was a fellow attached to the Queen's Men, Her Majesty's own troupe of players. And what did this man do during his forced hiatus? What else would a writer do, my lord. He wrote. The two long poems he penned are entitled *Venus and Adonis* and *The Rape of Lucrece*. And more importantly, they were printed with his name as author on the title pages. Both poems were dedicated to the 3rd Earl of Southhampton, who was one of Her Majesty's favorites at Court. Each poem also included a prefatory letter to the Earl, and both letters were signed "William Shakespeare." Yet, Sir Henry ignores these poems and the dedications completely. He and his clients would have us believe that these poems appeared by miraculous conception! Nay, my lord, they were written by the hand of William Shakespeare. There is no denying the evidence my lord, though there are those among us who will gladly do just that *(peering at Petitioner)*.

Item fourth, my lord. On 15 March 1595 Master Shakespeare is named as a payee in the Declared Accounts of the Treasurer of the

Royal Chamber, along with two others of the Lord Chamberlin's Men, with whom by this time he had joined, for, and I quote "two several comedies or interludes" during the Christmas past. While there is no record of which two comedies were then played, it is likely they were both attributed to Master Shakespeare because by this time he had become the Chamberlin's Men's resident playwright. Why else would he have been paid by the Queen's household? Petitioner is again, my lord, entirely silent on the subject.

Respondent

Item fifth, my lord. In 1595 and again in 1599 Master Skakespeare the writer is praised for his boundless talent by two prominent poets William Covell and John Weever, both of Cambridge, my lord. Weever's dedicatory poem to him is particularly effusive:

> *Honey-tongued Shakespeare, when I saw thine issue, I swore Apollo got them and none other, Their rosy-tainted featured clothed in tissue, Some heaven-born goddess said to be their mother.*

The evidence continues to mount, my lord.

Item sixth. In 1598 there appeared new quarto editions of three plays, *Richard the Second*, *Richard the Third* and *Love's Labour's Lost*, each specifically attributed by title pages to William Shakespeare. Again, this fact is entirely ignored by Sir Henry.

Petitioner:

With good reason, I can assure you, my lord.

Respondent:

Item seventh, my patient lord. That same year, 1598, appeared the literary work entitled *Palladis Tamia, Wit's Treasury*, by a prominent London critic named Francis Meres. In this small volume, which is a kind of collection of his thoughts on entertainments, Meres writes, and I quote:

"Shakespeare among the English is the most excellent (in comedy and tragedy) for the stage; for comedy witness his *Gentlemen of Verona*, his *Errors*, his *Love's Labour's Lost*, his *Love's Labour's Won*, his *Midsummer's Night Dream*, and his *Merchant of Venice;* for tragedy his *Richard the Second*, his *Richard the Third*, his *Henry the Fourth, King John, Titus Andronicus* and *Romeo and Juliet.*"

Meres also writes of Shakespeare and his lyric poetry, and again I quote: "...the most passionate among us to bewail and bemoan the perplexities of love."

If you've read his *Venus and Adonis,* my lord, you'd likely agree.

Judge:
Yes, yes. Are you almost finished, young Sparrow? I'm presently experiencing physical pain which might best be described as agony or torment. *(He palms his jaw once again.)*

Respondent:
Indeed I am, my lord.

Judge:
I am glad of it.

Respondent:
Item eighth is, my lord, the very significant documentary evidence furnished by various tax records from the City of London. I will not belabor the point, my lord, owing to your present distress. However, tax levies in 1599 and again in 1601 cite William Shakespeare as the occupant of The Globe theater, where, my lord, a dozen of his plays, at least, were performed before thousands.

Item ninth, my lord, and not an insignificant one if I dare say. In 1603, shortly after his arrival from Scotland, King James the First issued a royal patent naming William

Shakespeare, among others, as members of the King's troupe of players with license to perform plays in London and in the countryside. But as with the points above, Sir Henry again ignores this fact. He might as well ignore the sunrise, my lord.

And finally, my lord, is the tenth and final item I wish to present the court. That, of course, is the publication of the First Folio of his collected works, first printed in 1623 under the editorship of Henry Condell and John Heminge, who were Shakespeare's fellows with the King's Men. Their epistle "To the great variety of readers" is known only too well. After first explaining that the collection of these works by the author was denied them by his death, Masters Heminge and Condell state that they took the task upon themselves to offer the reader the plays in their original form due to the, and I quote: "...diverse stolen and surreptitious copies, maimed and deformed by the frauds and stealths of injurious impostors..." that were then available. You see, my lord, the printing practices of the age, so ably criticized by Sir Henry, corrupt as they may have been, issued at least fourteen plays attributed to Master Shakespeare during his lifetime, and another six after his death. His narrative poems *Venus* and *Lucrece,* previously described, enjoyed a total of nine printings during his lifetime and eight more following his demise. I offer this evidence parenthetically, my lord, to emphasize the import with which Heminge and Condell acted in preserving Master Shakespeare's plays for posterity.

And they continued, my lord, that these plays, thirty-six in number, and again I quote: "...are offered to your view cured and perfect of their limbs ... *(with emphasis in his voice)* as *he* conceived them." Further along, my lord, they wrote of Master Shakespeare, and I quote "Who, as he was a happy imitator of Nature, was a most gentle expresser of It. His mind and hand went together; and what he thought he uttered with that easiness, that we have scarce received from him a blot in his papers." There you have it, my lord, from the hand of those who knew him. They scarcely received a "blot in his papers!" *(He sneers at Petitioner.)* "*His* papers!"

Nor let us forget, as Sir Henry once again has, that no less a gentleman as the eminent poet and playwright Ben Jonson has written a dedicatory poem to Master Shakespeare, whom he calls therein, "Sweet swan of Avon." If you'll permit me, my lord, I will conclude my case with Jonson's own immortal words: *(He clears his throat.)*

> *Yet must I not give Nature all; thy Art, My gentle Shakespeare, must enjoy a part. For, though the poet's matter Nature be, His Art doth give the fashion; and that he Who casts to write a living line must sweat (Such as thine are) and strike the second heat Upon the Muses' anvil, turn the same (And himself with it) that he thinks to frame, Or the laurel he may gain a scorn; For a good poet's made as well as born.*

This my lord, is the final statement of my case, for how could I match the poetic skills of Ben Jonson, England's first poet laureate, and I might add, a personal acquaintance of Master Shakespeare? The foregoing ten items of evidence, my lord, each more convincing than the next, proves beyond doubt that William Shakespeare was indeed the author of the poems and plays attributed to him. I therefore respectfully rest my case, my lord, confident that this court will vindicate the reputation of this kingdom's greatest literary genius.

Judge:
Very well, Young Sparrow, nicely done. Will there be a rebuttal by the Petitioner Sir Henry?

Petitioner:
(Rising) Indeed there will be, my lord, for there must be, to correct the numerous erroneous inferences in Mr. Sparrow's summation of the so-called evidence.

Judge:
Then you'll be quick about, for both my benefit and that of the jury, who I might add, have been more than patient throughout these proceedings.

Petitioner:
I will straightaway to it, my lord. First, the so-called First Folio, upon which our young barrister places so much reliance, was in fact a hack job from beginning to end, my lord. It contains hundreds of errors, discrepancies, irregularities, blank and mis-numbered pages, and assorted corruptions. And why wouldn't it, my lord, for it was printed for profit and nothing else. Young Sparrow failed to mention that of the thirty-six plays contained therein, eighteen of them are attributed to William

Shakespeare for the very first time. In fact, they had never been printed before. I submit that these plays were included for the sole purpose of laying claim to them to the exclusion of all others who might rival the claim. How ingenious it was, to attribute them to Shakespeare, a man about which almost nothing is known. I submit, my lord, that this is exactly the case with all the plays: they were attributed to this man because he was a convenient lodger. It was an orchestrated subterfuge that served the surreptitious goals of the editors and publishers admirably well. I submit, my lord, that the name Shakespeare is in reality a noun of multitude.

Moreover, my lord, whosoever wrote the plays must have been a highly cultured man well-versed in languages, the classics, the law, politics, history, geography and many other areas of study. He has to have moved in the intimate circles of the aristocracy and have had knowledge of life at Court, in palaces and estates grand indeed. Yet there is absolutely no evidence in our young friend's presentation of the facts which remotely suggests Shaxper had such learning or such access. None whatsoever!

And that Ben Jonson was in on the scheme is made evident by the very low regard he appears to have held for this man Shakespeare. His dedicatory poem was written for money and for no other reason. After all, is it not still a common practice to pen such poems and prefaces in consideration for a fee? Of course it is. And why would Jonson write to honor the memory of a man he belittled, except for the money? Witness these lines written by Jonson of Shakespeare, my lord, as they are more telling than any recited by Young Sparrow:

> *Poor poet-player, that would be thought our chief Whose works are even the frippery of wit, From brokerage is become so bold a thieve, As we, the robbed, leave rage, and pity it.*
> *At first he made low shifts, would pick and glean, Buy the reversion of old plays, now grown To a little wealth and credit in the scene, He takes up all, makes each man's wit his own, And told of this, he slights it.*
> *Fool! As if half eyes will not know a reece From locks of wool or shreds from the whole piece.*

Thus did Ben Jonson think of Shakespeare. He was a literary thief who converted the works of others, and then had the temerity to call them his own. And since when, my lord, did attribution prove authorship? Under the conditions prevailing at the time, attribution of authorship meant nothing at all. In the interest of time, my lord, I will forgo offering numerous examples of false attributions of authorship, many of which involved Master Shakespeare himself. It is no answer to the question at hand, my lord, to say that Shakespeare wrote the plays because his name appears on the title pages or because the plays were registered by various printers as his. The only true proof would be evidence from Shakespeare himself, and no such evidence has been offered. Indeed, it could not be offered because it simply does not exist.

Nor is there evidence that Shakespeare himself ever claimed the plays as his own, nor any interest in the theaters he is supposed to have owned in part. His last will and testament are completely silent in this regard. This is in marked contrast to the evidence of Master Shaxper of Stratford, who inventoried his estate down to his "second best bed."

I submit, my lord, that the mystery here is not who wrote the plays, but how the identity of this Shaxper of Stratford became confused with that of Shakespeare of the London stage? Indeed, I doubt it is in our power to solve this mystery, my lord, because many clever men took pains to devise it so as to deceive posterity about the authorship. This was done in the name of greed, my lord, which makes their motives highly suspect. It is to their clever ruse, and to their sublime artifice, that we owe this controversy. And that controversy is: Did Shaxper write the plays and the poems attributed to Shakespeare? I submit that he did not, that there is no way he could have written them, and that Respondent's claim is but the bitter fruit of the skullduggery I have described. I repeat, we bear no ill-will to Sir John or his wife, Lady Bernard. Indeed, we think it an indignation that their good name has been thus profaned. In the end, my lord, we must admit what is plainly true: That there is no evidence that this man from Stratford was a writer of anything at all.

Thank you, my gracious lord. *(He steps away from his lectern, full of himself for what he regards as a fine performance.)*

Judge:
That will suffice then; the court will charge the jury to render its verdict... aggahhhh!.

Respondent:
I beg your pardon, my lord, there is one matter more which I beg leave to present in counter-rebuttal to Sir Henry.

Judge:
And what would that be?

Respondent:
Sir Henry has leveled a charge which has no merit, and to leave uncontroverted would result in a travesty of justice.

Judge:
And what would that be, counsel?

Respondent:
The suggestion that Shakespeare of Stratford and Shakespeare of London were two different persons.

Judge:
I see....

Petitioner:
My lord, there is no evidence they were the same....

Respondent:

There you are wrong, Sir Henry. For in the chancel of Holy Trinity Church in Stratford is mounted a monument to William Shakespeare, the one and only. He is portrayed in bust with a plume in his hand. The inscription praises him for his gift of writing. This is of paramount importance, my lord, as it proves incontrovertibly the connection between, as Sir Henry has fashioned, "Shaxper and Shakespeare." If there is a deception, it is not one that was created then, but now. Sir Henry's clients have a direct pecuniary interest in the outcome of these proceedings. Nothing would please them more than to print and reprint Master Shakespeare's plays for the sole purpose of selling them at a profit and without contributing the legal share to the rightful claimant. Despite all of Sir Henry's arguments, he has not offered a single piece of proof as to who other than William Shakespeare wrote the poems and plays. This is because there is no proof as to any other authors. That William Shakespeare was a literary genius is uncontroverted, whether or not he moved in high places. For genius is not an occupation, my lord, but a gift of Nature. I submit, my lord, that however improbable Sir Henry believes William Shakespeare's genius was, it cannot be denied him, nor should it be, if England is a just kingdom which honors the memory of her most illustrious sons. That is all, my lord. That is my case. I urge the court, and you, ladies and gentlemen of the jury, to look favorably upon Lady Bernard's claim. Thank you, my lord. *(He stands aside.)*

Judge:

Very good, then, both parties have rested. I'll instruct the jury so they can render their verdict. Toby, is the charge ready?

Clerk:

It is, my lord. I have it here, your lordship. *(He hands the judge a document.)*

Judge:

(To the audience.)

Ladies and gentlemen of the jury: You have listened attentively to the evidence. It is now your duty to consider it in answering the central question: Did Lady Bernard's maternal grandfather, no matter the pronunciation of his name, write the plays and poems attributed to the great William Shakespeare? Please consider your opinion carefully. When you have resolved upon the question, you will then be asked to raise your hands to signal your vote as cast. I trust this is clear. Toby, I will retire until you summon me. *(He stands and descends the dais, exiting while holding his jaw in pain.)*

Agghhhhh.......!!!

Clerk:

(Standing) Ladies and gentlemen of the jury, as his lordship described, you will decide the central question. You may now have a moment to reflect upon the evidence. I bid you will do so thoughtfully and honorably. The gravity of these proceedings demands nothing less!

He seats himself at his desk in front of the bench, and takes up some documents for study. The lights over him subside. Taking this as their cue, the two barristers enter among the audience to prod, plead and cajole audience members to vote in their favor. This is an opportunity for light comedies. After a minute, the lights come up over the clerk. He then looks up and says:

I will now summon his lordship for the verdict.

The barristers quickly return to their podiums, and resume a measure of decorum. The Clerk then rises and rings a hand bell to summon the judge.

All rise.

The Judge enters and takes the bench.

Judge:
Is the jury prepared to render its verdict?

Clerk:
It is, your lordship.

Judge:
Then let's have it without further delay. Are the parties ready for the presentation of the verdict?

Petitioner:
I am, my lord.

Respondent:
Ready, my lord. We have been ready for years!

Judge:
Ladies and gentlemen of the jury. In a moment I will ask you to cast your vote. It is incumbent upon each of you to refrain from looking around the room to view your neighbors' votes. It is mandatory that each of you vote your own conscience, based upon the evidence submitted. Is this perfectly clear to all of you? Good! With that said, each of you who believes the late William Shakespeare in fact wrote the

plays and poems attributed to him during his lifetime and afterwards will please raise your hands. *(The clerk counts the raised hands.)* Each of you who believes there is sufficient grounds to doubt his authorship will please now raise their hands. *(Again, the clerk makes a count.)*

(To himself.) Very interesting. The clerk will prepare a verdict ballot and deliver it to me.

The Clerk hurriedly marks the ballot and hands it to the Judge.

Clerk:
Here it is, your lordship.

Judge:
(He reads the verdict ballot.) We, the people of the jury, hereby and in favor of: choose one

( ) Petitioner

( ) Respondent

In either case, the judge gestures to the prevailing party. That party reacts victoriously. The defeated party reacts with anger and disappointment.

Clerk:
Ladies and gentlemen of the jury, I humbly thank you for your time and participation. If

you'll permit me, I will conclude our affairs together in reciting a favorite adage of mine about the law. It is thus: the law is principally concerned with a search for the truth; Truth is principally concerned with the ideal of justice. Unfortunately, neither truth nor justice are principal concerns of the law despite what we are led to believe. If our experience has taught us anything it is this: Man will see what he wants to see, and he will fight to the end his right to describe what he saw. When another man who likewise saw it, sees it differently, he will likewise fight for the triumph of his vision. That is why a civilized society settles disputes in accordance with the ability of each contestant to prove exactly what he saw to an unbiased judge or jury. You have seen this process played out before you. Whether it has need played out correctly—or played well—is a matter upon which people of good faith can and will disagree. Yet it is better that they do so than that they shouldn't care. Otherwise we would find ourselves forever perched on the edge of uncertainty, reluctant to enact law, discern truth or seek justice. I trust the proceedings have been enlightening for you. Having fulfilled your duty with uncommon excellence, you are hereby discharged. I bid you each a good day and trust you are enjoying your visit to our fair city.

Lights go down. **The judge, Clerk and both barristers exit.** *Once off stage, the judge lets out a final groan of pain, "Agggghhhhhhhh..."*

Finis

About the Author

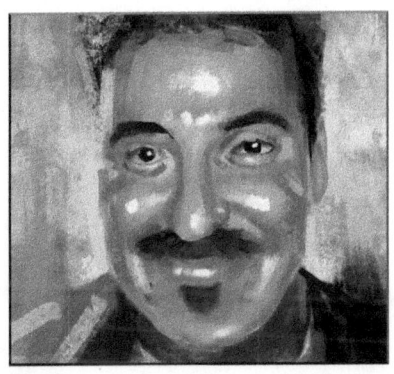

Joseph S. Ajlouny is an attorney, agent and writer from Detroit. His many plays include *The Trial of William Shakespeare*, *The Red Poppy: Joseph Stalin at Home*, and *Marilyn, Norma Jean and Me*. He is also the author of more than a dozen humor and popular reference books under the pen name Joey West.

Joseph is director of The Federal Bureau of Entertainment, a production company that specializes in the development and presentation of one-person shows.

Production History

The Trial of William Shakespeare premiered at The Queen's Inn, Stratford, Ontario on June 3, 1997. The script was developed by the playwright as a consequence of his having been invited to "litigate" the issue in a fund-raising event sponsored by the Kent County (Michigan) Bar Association the year before. He was not unmindful of the fact that timeless questions raised in The Bard's writings have been resolved in courtroom settings such as we have here. Mr. Ajlouny has participated, coached or judged in litigious dramatizations of the sanity of Hamlet, the murder of the young princes and the merits of the grievances of the Montagues and Capulets.

The play premiered on The Arena Stage Stratford-Upon-Avon in July 1997. It has since been performed in theatres, college classrooms and Shakespeare festivals in over a dozen countries.

Prop List:

Set:

1. Bench and chair for Judge; bench covered with red satin cloth and appropriate knickknacks.
2. Desk and chair for Clerk
3. Two podiums for Barristers

Costumes:

1. Three white wigs for Judge and Barristers; one red wig for Clerk
2. Appropriate robes for Judge and Barristers; suit for Clerk

Props:

1. Feather duster
2. Quill pen
3. Gavel
4. Easel and pointing stick
5. Sign reading "Marlowe was gay."
6. Handbell
7. Stack of papers (documents)
8. Verdict ballot

Exhibits:

Poster listing the ten proofs offered by Sparrow:
  i. Robert Greene's attack 1592
  ii. Henry Chettle's apology 1592
  iii. Narrative poems 1593
  iv. Royal Chamber Accounts 1595
  v. Praise by Covell and Weever 1595/99
  vi. Title Page attributions 1598
  vii. Meres' *Palladis Tamia* 1598
  viii. Tax levies on The Globe 1599/1601
  ix. Royal Patent — King's Men 1603
  x. First Folio 1623

Additional Items Needed:
  1. Recording of stoic male voice reading Sonnet 81, played onto set
  2. Stage microphones and sound system
  3. Appropriate overhead lighting

Fresh Ink Group

Publishing
Free Memberships
Share & Read Free Stories, Essays, Articles
Free-Story Newsletter
Writing Contests

⁂

Books
E-books
Amazon Bookstore

⁂

Authors
Editors
Artists
Professionals
Publishing Services
Publisher Resources

⁂

Members' Websites
Members' Blogs
Social Media

Email: info@FreshInkGroup.com
Twitter: @FreshInkGroup
Google+: Fresh Ink Group
Facebook.com/FreshInkGroup
LinkedIn: Fresh Ink Group
About.me/FreshInkGroup
FreshInkGroup.com

MARILYN, NORMA JEAN AND ME

In this boisterous but sensitive drama, playwright J. Ajlouny looks beyond public image to find the heart of this young woman thrust wildly into fame as a sex symbol. Presented as a play-in-the-making within a play, *Marilyn, Norma Jean and Me* weaves biography with humor to explore the movie star's widely speculated desire to leave Hollywood for Broadway. The author imagines her innocence and vulnerability, her friendliness and loyalty, even as the public image threatens to steal her humanity. This play is a masterpiece, not just because it is so good, but for its powerful way of finding the real Norma Jean in the legend known as Marilyn Monroe.

PUSH PULL PRESS / Fresh Ink Group

Meet William Shakespeare

Much has been explored about Shakespeare and his life, but little is known about how this small-town boy with a grammar-school education came to pen masterworks like *Hamlet* and *King Lear*. In *Meet William Shakespeare*, playwright J. Ajlouny creates authentic and plausible explanations that answer centuries-old questions about the man and his work. The result is an educational and fun portrait of Shakespeare, as told by The Bard himself.

PUSH PULL PRESS / Fresh Ink Group

WHO SAID THAT?

Who Said That? provides an entertaining and authoritative reference for the origins and meanings of our common figures of speech.

- Who said 100+ famous expressions?
- Who *really* said them?
- What did they actually say?
- What did they actually mean?
- Why did they say them that way?
- Who repeated what was said?

Surprisingly true, sometimes strange, always fascinating, the stories about whence came these expressions will entertain, educate, and even amaze you.

Fresh Ink Group

FIGURATIVELY SPEAKING

A figure of speech is an expression in which the words are used, but not in their literal sense, to create a more forceful or dramatic meaning. They are often in the form of metaphors, similes and hyperbole. "A fountain of knowledge," is a good example. "Stretching the truth," is another.

With Figuratively Speaking, we finally have a thesaurus to discover these phrases' origins and the sources of their meanings. Categories include:Attitudes, Body Types, Competition, Creature Comforts, Letting Loose, Ethics, Influence, Life-Health-Death, Money, Personal Space, Personality Types, Speech, Thinking Power, Time, Trouble-Turmoil-Commotion, and The World of Work. Whether reading it for fun, researching phrases you use, or studying the symbolic foundations of our language, Figuratively Speaking is the resource you'll reach for time and again.

Fresh Ink Group

www.ingramcontent.com/pod-product-compliance
Lightning Source LLC
Chambersburg PA
CBHW071413040426
42444CB00009B/2227